"Branch Topped or Round" Branching or Rounding the serif

?CIJV ?L ?S ?XY

RRTTUU

VUX X 3 ?2 3

Flourished

Drawing out (of flourishing) any Strokes

BAA#A

BEFEF

FGHHJJ

JKLL

Denis Wheatley 1967.

A Book of Sample Scripts

Edward Johnston

VICTORIA AND ALBERT MUSEUM

EDWARD JOHNSTON

The House of David, his Inheritance: A Book of Sample Scripts 1914 A.D.

LONDON: HER MAJESTY'S STATIONERY OFFICE

1966

Introduction

EDWARD Johnston's *Book of Sample Scripts*, here reproduced in facsimile, is perhaps the outstanding manuscript of a calligrapher whose genius both as artist and teacher has profoundly influenced lettering design in Great Britain and abroad throughout the present century. The manuscript owes its origin to Sir Sydney Cockerell (d. 1962), sometime Director of the Fitzwilliam Museum, Cambridge, who privately commissioned, in 1913, an example of Johnston's work. Under the title of *The House of David, his Inheritance: a Book of Sample Scripts* the manuscript was completed in March 1914. It comprises a series of Biblical texts relating to King David in Greek, Latin and English, chosen by Johnston and written out on vellum in black and red letters in a variety of scripts. A list and description of the different hands is given at the end of the manuscript (page 31); together they form a masterly series of sample scripts for students of fine lettering.

Edward Johnston was born in Uruguay, of Quaker stock, on 11th February 1872 and died at Ditchling, Sussex, on 26th November 1944. After studying medicine for a short time at Edinburgh University he abandoned a medical career in 1897 on account of ill health, devoting himself thenceforth to the study and practice of calligraphy. For many years he taught lettering in London at the Central School of Arts and Crafts and at the Royal College of Art. His script was based primarily on the formal book hand used in manuscripts of the 'Winchester' school of illumination during the tenth and eleventh centuries; in later life he adopted a more angular, current style, which owed something to the decorative and expressive qualities of the later Gothic scripts. In 1906 he published *Writing & Illuminating, & Lettering*, an indispensable manual for the scribe, and in 1909 *Manuscript and Inscription Letters*. Though primarily a calligrapher, Johnston also concerned himself with typography. Between 1910–30 he designed calligraphic founts for Count Harry Kessler, of the Cranach Press, Weimar, but his most important commission came in 1916 from Frank Pick, Managing Director of the Underground Group of Railways in London. This was to design special alphabets for the exclusive use of London's Underground and its associated companies. The resulting Johnston sans serif type, based on the proportions of the classical Roman capital letter, is still used for official signs and notices throughout the London Transport system.

Johnston's pioneer work in the rediscovery of the technique and structure of letter-forms was the primary source of the modern revival of interest in better writing. The *Book of Sample Scripts* was, indeed, already in existence when Mr Stanley Morison wrote in 1926 (*Type Designs of the Past and Present*, page 64) 'Perhaps Mr Johnston will one day give us . . . a new copy book to teach us hands which we can write without recourse to quill pens and indian ink.'

The *Book of Sample Scripts* was presented to the Museum in 1959 by Sir Sydney Cockerell, the first President of the William Morris Society, who contributed greatly, by his sustained interest and active encouragement, to the Library's calligraphic collections. The manuscript is now reproduced with the kind permission of Mr Johnston's daughters, Mrs Priscilla Roworth and Miss Bridget Johnston.

Mr Johnston's numbering of the written pages has been preserved in the facsimile production. In the original manuscript, his title page (page 5), is preceded by four otherwise blank pages numbered 1 to 4. Likewise, at the end of the original work, four pages, otherwise blank, were numbered by him as pages 33 to 36.

December 1965

J. P. HARTHAN
Keeper of the Library
Victoria & Albert Museum

AABCDEFGHIJKLMNO

et divisit Lucem a tenebris.

OPQRSTUVWXY

Appellavitque Lucem Diem et

The House of David,
his Inheritance:
A
book of sample scripts
1914. A.D.

et est vespere et mane, dies unus.

OPQRSTUVWXYZ

Et tenebras Noctem: factumq.

VABCDEFGHIJKLMNO

THE CONTENTS

ΚΑΙΛΕΓΕΙ,
ΓΡΑΨΟΝ·ΟΤΙΟΥΤΟΙΟΙΛΟΓΟΙ
ΠΙCΤΟΙΚΑΙΑΛΗΘΙΝΟΙΕΙCΙ.
ΚΑΙΕΙΠΕΜΟΙ,ΓΕΓΟΝΑΝ.
ΕΓΩΤΟΑΚΑΙΤΟΩ,
ΗΑΡΧΗΚΑΙΤΟΤΕΛΟC.
ΕΓΩΤΩΙΔΙΨΩΝΤΙ
ΔΩCCΩΕΚΤΗCΠΗΓΗC
ΤΟΥΥΔΑΤΟCΤΗCΖΩΗC
ΔΩΡΕΑΝ.ΟΝΙΚΩΝ
ΚΛΗΡΟΝΟΜΗCΕΙΤΑΥΤΑ,
ΚΑΙΕCΟΜΑΙΑΥΤΩΙΘΕΟC,
ΚΑΙΑΥΤΟCΕCΤΑΙΜΟΙΥΙΟC.

7

The Story of David and Goliath : from the first Book of Samuel.

NOW the Philistines gathered together their armies to battle, and they were gathered together at Socoh, which belongeth to Judah, and pitched between Socoh and Azekah, in Ephes-dammim. And Saul and the men of Israel were gathered together, and pitched in the vale of Elah, and set the battle in array against the Philistines. And the Philistines stood on the mountain on the one side, and Israel stood on the mountain on the other side: and there was a valley between them. And there went out a champion out of the camp of the Philistines, named Goliath, of Gath, whose height was six cubits and a span. And he had an helmet of brass upon his head, and he was clad with a coat of mail; and the weight of the coat was five thousand shekels of brass. And he had greaves of brass upon his legs, and a javelin of brass between his shoulders. And the staff of his spear was like a weaver's beam; and his spear's head weighed six hundred shekels of iron: and his shield-bearer went before him. And he stood and cried unto the armies of Israel, and said unto them, Why are ye come out to set your battle in array? am not I a Philistine, and ye servants to Saul? choose you a man for you, and let him come down to me. If he be able to fight with me, and kill me, then will we be your servants: but if I prevail against him, and kill him, then shall ye be our servants, and serve us. And the Philistine said, I DEFY THE ARMIES OF ISRAEL THIS DAY; GIVE ME A MAN, THAT WE MAY FIGHT TOGETHER. And when Saul and all Israel heard those words of the Philistine, they were dismayed and greatly afraid. ——※——※——※——※——※——

NOW David was the son of that Ephrathite of Beth-lehem-judah, whose name was Jesse; and he had eight sons: and the man was an old man in the days of Saul, stricken in years among men. And the three eldest sons of Jesse had gone after Saul to the battle: and the names of his three sons

that went to the battle were Eliab the first-
born, and next unto him Abinadab, and the
third Shammah. And David was the young-
est: and the three eldest followed Saul. Now
David went to and fro from Saul to feed his
father's sheep at Beth-lehem. And the Philistine drew near morning and evening, and
presented himself forty days.————※——※

AND JESSE SAID UNTO DAVID
HIS SON, Take now for thy brethren an
ephah of this parched corn, and these ten
loaves, and carry *them* quickly to the camp
to thy brethren; and bring these ten cheeses
unto the captain of their thousand, and
look how thy brethren fare, and take their

pledge. Now Saul, and they, and all the men of Israel, were in the vale of Elah, fighting with the Philistines. And David rose up early in the morning, and left the sheep with a keeper, and took, and went, as Jesse had commanded him; and he came to the place of the wagons, as the host which was going forth to the fight shouted for the battle. And Israel and the Philistines put the battle in array, army against army. And David left his baggage in the hand of the keeper of the baggage, and ran to the army, and came and saluted his brethren. And as he talked with them, behold, there came up the champion, the Philistine of Gath, Goliath by name, out of the ranks of

13

the Philistines, and spake according to the same words: and David heard them. And all the men of Israel, when they saw the man, fled from him, and were sore afraid. And the men of Israel said, Have ye seen this man that is come up? surely to defy Israel is he come up: and it shall be, that the man who killeth him, the king will enrich him with great riches, and will give him his daughter, and make his father's house free in Israel. And David spake to the men that stood by him, saying, What shall be done to the man that killeth this Philistine, and taketh away the reproach from Israel? for who is this uncircumcised Philistine, that he should defy the armies of the living God? And the people answered him after this manner, saying, So shall it be done to the man that killeth him. And Eliab his eldest brother heard when he spake unto the men; and Eliab's anger was kindled against David, and he said, Why art thou come down? and with whom hast thou left those few sheep in the wilderness? I know thy pride, and the naughtiness of thine heart; for thou art come down that thou mightest see the battle. And David said, What have I now done? Is there not a cause? And he turned away from him toward another, and spake after the same manner: and the people answered him again

15

after the former manner. And when the words were heard which David spake, they rehearsed them before Saul; and he sent for him. And David said to Saul, Let no man's heart fail because of him; thy servant will go and fight with this Philistine. And Saul said to David, Thou art not able to go against this Philistine to fight with him: for thou art but a youth, and he a man of war from his youth. And David said unto Saul, Thy servant kept his father's sheep; and when there came a lion, or a bear, and took a lamb out of the flock, I went out after him, and smote him, and delivered it out of his mouth: and when he arose against me, I caught him by his beard, and smote him, and slew him. Thy servant smote both the lion and the bear: and this uncircumcised Philistine shall be as one of them, seeing he hath defied the armies of the living God. And David said, The Lord that delivered me out of the paw of the lion, and out of the paw of the bear, he will deliver me out of the hand of this Philistine. And Saul said unto David, Go, and the Lord shall be with thee. And Saul clad David with his apparel, and he put an helmet of brass upon his head, and he clad him with a coat of mail. And David girded his sword upon his apparel, and he assayed to go; for he had not proved it. And David

17

said unto Saul, I cannot go with these;
for I have not proved them. And David
put them off him. And he took his staff
in his hand, and chose him five smooth
stones out of the brook, and put them in
the shepherd's bag which he had, even in
his scrip; and his sling was in his hand:
and he drew near to the Philistine. And
the Philistine came on and drew near unto
David; and the man that bare the shield
went before him. And when the Philistine
looked about, and saw David, he disdained
him: for he was but a youth, and ruddy,
and withal of a fair countenance. And the
Philistine said unto David, Am I a dog,
that thou comest to me with staves? And

the Philistine cursed David by his gods. And the Philistine said to David, COME TO ME, AND I WILL GIVE THY FLESH UNTO THE FOWLS OF THE AIR, AND TO THE BEASTS OF THE FIELD. Then said David to the Philistine, Thou comest to me with a sword, and with a spear, and with a javelin: but I come to thee in the name of the Lord of hosts, the God of the armies of Israel, which thou hast defied. This day will the Lord deliver thee into mine hand; and I will smite thee, and take thine head from off thee; and I will give the carcases of the host of the Philistines this day unto the fowls of the air, and to the wild beasts of

19.

the earth; that all the earth may know that there is a God in Israel: and that all this assembly may know that the Lord saveth not with sword and spear: for the battle is the LORD'S, and he will give you into our hand. And it came to pass, when the Philistine arose, and came and drew nigh to meet David, that David hastened, and ran toward the army to meet the Philistine. And David put his hand in his bag, and took thence a stone, and slang it, and smote the Philistine in his forehead; and the stone sank into his forehead, and he fell upon his face to the earth. So David prevailed over the Philistine with a sling and with a stone, and smote the Philistine, and slew him; but there was no sword in the hand of David. Then David ran, and stood over the Philistine, and took his sword, and drew it out of the sheath thereof, and slew him, and cut off his head therewith. And when the Philistines saw that their champion was dead, they fled. And the men of Israel and of Judah arose, and shouted, and pursued the Philistines, until thou comest to Gai, and to the gates of Ekron. And the wounded of the Philistines fell down by the way to Shaaraim, even unto Gath, and unto Ekron. And the children of Israel returned from chasing after the Philistines, and they spoiled their camp. And David took the head of the Philistine, and brought it to Jerusalem; but he put his armour in his tent.

21

A Psalm of David.

The LORD is my shepherd;
I shall not want.
He maketh me to lie down
in green pastures:
He leadeth me beside
the ¹still waters.

1. Heb. waters of rest.

He restoreth my soul:
He guideth me in the paths of
righteousness for his name's sake.
Yea, though I walk through the
valley of ²the shadow of death,
I will fear no evil;

2. Or, deep darkness.

for thou art with me:
Thy rod and thy staff,
they comfort me.
Thou preparest a table before me
in the presence of mine enemies:
Thou hast anointed my head
with oil; my cup runneth over.
Surely goodness and mercy shall
follow me all the days of my life:
And I will dwell in the house of
the LORD⁴ for ever

3. Or, only

4. Heb. for length of days.

23

OUR fathers had the tabernacle of the testimony in the wilderness, even as he appointed who spake unto Moses, that he should make it according to the figure that he had seen. Which also our fathers, in their turn, brought in with Joshua when they entered on the possession of the nations, which God thrust out before the face of our fathers, unto the days of David; who found favour in the sight of God, and asked to find a habitation for the God of Jacob. But Solomon built him a house. Howbeit the Most

High dwelleth not in houses made
with hands; as saith the prophet,
The heaven is my
    throne,
And the earth the foot-
stool of my feet:
What manner of house
    will ye build me ?
saith the Lord:
Or what is the place of
    my rest ?
Did not my hand make
    all these things ?

Acts, vij, 44-50.

Dignus es, Domine Deus noster, accipere gloriam, et honorem, et virtutem:
quia tu creasti omnia, et propter vo-
luntatem tuam erant, et creata sunt.
And I saw in the right hand of
him that sat on the throne a
book written within and on the
back, close sealed with seven
seals. And I saw a strong angel
proclaiming with a great voice,
Who is worthy to open the book,
and to loose the seals thereof ?
And no one in the heaven, or on

the earth, or under the earth, was able to open the book, or to look thereon. And I wept much, because no one was found worthy to open the book, or to look thereon: and one of the elders saith unto me, Weep not: behold, the Lion that is of the tribe of Judah, the Root of David, hath overcome, to open the book and the seven seals thereof. And I saw in the midst of the throne

27

and of the four living creatures,
and in the midst of the elders, a
Lamb standing, as though it
had been slain, having seven horns,
and seven eyes, which are the seven Spirits of God, sent forth into all the earth. And he came,
and he taketh *it* out of the right
hand of him that sat on the throne.
And when he had taken the book,
the four living creatures and the
four and twenty elders fell down

before the Lamb, having each one a harp, and golden bowls full of incense, which are the prayers of the saints. And they sing a new song, saying, Dignus es, Domine, accipere librum, et aperire signacula ejus: quoniam occisus es, et redemisti nos Deo in sanguine tuo ex omni tribu, et lingua, et populo, et natione: et fecisti nos Deo nostro regnum, et sacerdotes: et regnabimus super terram. ✠ ✠ ✠ SEDENTI IN THRONO, et Agno, benedictio, et honor, et gloria, et potestas, in saecula saeculorum.

℞ Amen

29

ET OSTENDIT MIHI FLVVIVM
AQVAE VITAE, SPLENDIDVM
TAMQVAM CRYSTALLVM,
PROCEDENTEM DE SEDE
DEI ET AGNI.
IN MEDIO PLATEAE EIVS, ET
EX VTRAQVE PARTE FLVMI-
NIS LIGNVM VITAE, AFFERENS
FRVCTVS DVODECIM, PER MEN-
SES SINGVLOS REDDENS FRVC-
TVM SVVM, ET FOLIA LIGNI
AD SANITATEM GENTIVM.

This Book contains 36 pp. of vellum & 2 parchment ends.
The Sample Scripts used in it are —
pp. 8-21. The "foundational hand" based on 10. Century English MS.
pp. 22, 23, 5. "Black Italic" } formed from the above.
pp. 26-29. "Small roman" }
pp. 24-25 { "Modern half-uncial" } based on round skeleton forms
{ "Uncials" to match. } approximated to Uncial character
used by the Writer as an educational hand since 1900 A.D.
p. 30. "Roman Capital MS." based on Sq. Caps. of 3. or 4. Centy. or 5.
There are also various pen-made Roman Capitals
in the Title Page and in other places.
E J, the Writer; I record with regret erasures occurring on pp. 17. 23. 27. 31.
these pp. should have been rewritten but I promised
to finish the book by Lady day. (Note: the roughness
of the Vellum in other places is due to the manner of
preparing it) . The caps on pp. 11. 12. are not quite happy,
but as to a word here and there the Writer nearly is. F
Finished 24 Mar. [in 1914 A . D .
no
mine
E. J.]

31

Printed and published by
HER MAJESTY'S STATIONERY OFFICE

Printed in England

for abc & kindred Book Hands

A A A A B C C D E
"CROSS TOPPED or Square" Stiffening or Squaring the Form

E F C G G G I H H I
J J R L M M N
N N N O O P
Q Q Q Q Q R
R S T U V W W
X X X Y Y Z
u v w x 22